The Day-Glo Brothers

The True Story of Bob and Joe Switzer's
Bright Ideas and Brand-New Colors

CHRIS BARTON

Illustrated by **TONY PERSIANI**

ini Charlesbridge

To my brilliant, dazzling wife, Casey, and our vibrant
sons, Sage and Fletcher—C. B.

In memory of John, a great artist but better friend, and
to my precious daughter Chloe for what lies ahead—T. P.

Published by Charlesbridge
85 Main Street
Watertown, MA 02472
(617) 926-0329
www.charlesbridge.com

Library of Congress Cataloging-in-Publication Data
Barton, Chris.
    The Day-Glo brothers / Chris Barton ; illustrated by Tony Persiani.
        p. cm.
    ISBN 978-1-57091-673-1 (reinforced for library use)
1. Fluorescence—Juvenile literature. 2. Colors—Juvenile literature.
3. Paint—Juvenile literature. I. Title.
QC477.B29 2009
535'.352—dc22   2008026959

Printed in the United States of America
(hc) 10 9 8 7 6 5 4 3 2 1

Display type and text type set in Humper and Knock Out
Color separated, printed, and bound by Lake Book Manufacturing, Inc.
Production supervision by Brian G. Walker
Designed by Susan Mallory Sherman

Even if they'd wanted to, the ancient Egyptians couldn't have painted their pyramids a green that glowed in the desert sun. Back in 2600 BCE, there was no such color.

A glowing orange Statue of Liberty might have made coming to America even more memorable. But when Lady Liberty was assembled in 1886, that color wasn't an option.

And in 1920, if young Bob and Joe Switzer had thought their family's Montana cottage would look better with a yellow glow, they would have been out of luck, too.

But not for long. After all, it was the Switzer brothers themselves who would soon bring those eye-popping yellows, oranges, and greens into the world. It would just take a few bright ideas.

The Switzer brothers' illuminating tale begins with Bob, born in 1914.
From early on, Bob loved to work. He earned money shoveling snow,
picking beets, and using a souped-up Model T Ford to round up wild
horses. Bob wasn't just a worker; he was a planner, too. One summer he
saved his money to pay for a ride in the open cockpit of a stunt plane at
the fair in Billings.

Joe, younger by fifteen months, exerted himself a lot less than his older brother—practicing magic tricks was more his speed. With his knack for sleight of hand, he made metal rings and playing cards seem to disappear and reappear.

Joe also had a problem-solving streak. His dad had kidney trouble and a bad back, so Joe rigged a mirror allowing Mr. Switzer to lie down at the back of his drugstore and still watch for customers coming through the front door.

A long drought brought hard times to Montana, so in 1931 the family moved to Berkeley, California, where Mr. Switzer had bought a pharmacy.

In Berkeley Joe began wowing crowds with magic shows at school and church. His act included a kind of illusion called black art. Black art involved an object, painted half black and half white, that seemed to float and then disappear when held and turned under a white spotlight in front of a black background.

It was a nifty trick, but Joe wished he could make it even better.

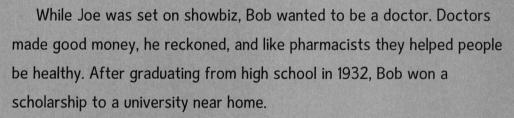

While Joe was set on showbiz, Bob wanted to be a doctor. Doctors made good money, he reckoned, and like pharmacists they helped people be healthy. After graduating from high school in 1932, Bob won a scholarship to a university near home.

In 1933 Bob took a summer job inspecting railroad cars at a gigantic pickle and ketchup factory. One day when Bob was climbing into a car full of ketchup bottles, the barricade he was standing on collapsed. Bob fell about twelve feet and hit his head on the concrete loading dock.

The fall gave Bob seizures and double vision. It damaged his memory and ended his plan to become a doctor. Bob had to spend several months at home healing in the darkened basement.

Joe was down there, too, but for a different reason. He was in the dark so he could think about light. Joe had read in *Popular Science* about ultraviolet lamps, also called black lights, which made certain substances glow in the dark.

Joe knew this glow, called fluorescence, could jazz up his magic act. The dim basement where Bob was stuck recovering seemed like the perfect place to experiment.

Bob was bored and eager to help.

Together the brothers built their own ultraviolet lamp.
One night they took it into their dad's drugstore.
In the darkened storeroom, they aimed
the light at the bottles and boxes
on the shelves.

There in the dark, the chemical-stained label on a bottle of eyewash
emitted a yellow glow.

That glow lit up the Switzers' imaginations. They brought home lots of books from the library and began learning how to use different chemicals to make glow-in-the-dark paints. In regular light they looked plain, but under the ultraviolet light they radiated bright, attention-getting colors.

Bob thought they could use the paint for more than just Joe's magic act. They could sell it for use in store-window displays and make a little money to help cover Bob's medical bills.

Bob and Joe scrounged around the university and other local labs for additional fluorescent materials. When they got hold of some—say, uranine, or anthracene—they ground them with their father's mortar and pestle. Then they secretly used their mother's new kitchen mixer to combine the powders with alcohol, shellac, or other ingredients.

The results? Splattering, gooey, glowing paints. And once, when Mrs. Switzer surprised them before they could clean all the paint out of the mixer, a peculiar-looking angel food cake.

But Bob and Joe had a bigger problem: the sun. The effect of ultraviolet light was impossible to see in daylight. Plus, the sunlight faded the paints so that they wouldn't glow at night, either. So much for Joe and Bob using their paints in store windows.

While they were wrong about that idea, Joe was right about how fluorescence could boost his magic act. In his "Balinese dancer" illusion, a woman wore a fluorescent-painted paper costume. While she cavorted on a stage lit only by an ultraviolet lamp, Joe—unseen by the audience— yanked off her headdress. The dancer went one way, and her "head" went the other!

It was a gruesome effect, but it won first prize at a magicians' convention and made the newspaper. Word got around, and soon Joe and Bob had lots of customers.

The Warfield Theater bought fluorescent costumes that made chorus girls look like wriggling skeletons.

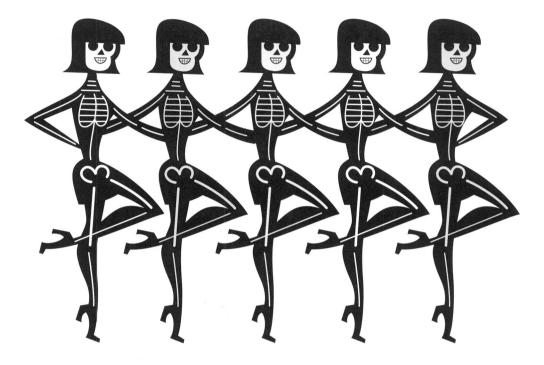

The toy department at Hale Brothers featured a glow-in-the-dark Christmas display.

"Spiritualists" used the brothers' paint to trick gullible customers into thinking they were seeing ghosts of their dearly departed loved ones.

A printer in Cleveland, Ohio, began using the Switzer boys' fluorescent ink to make posters for movie theaters. Like the rest of Joe and Bob's creations, the ink in those posters was used mostly inside and glowed only under ultraviolet light.

But one day in May 1935, while Joe was away drumming up more business, Bob made a curious discovery. He had dipped some silk fabric samples in a boiling combination of alcohol and fluorescent dye. Then he hung the samples in the backyard to see whether sunlight would fade this latest concoction.

A little while later Bob was in the front yard when something caught his eye. Even at that distance—and in ordinary daylight—he could see that the fabric in the backyard was glowing.

What had caused this? The alcohol? The dye? The boiling? The silk? Bob didn't know, and with a million things on their minds, he and Joe didn't have time to figure out the answer—not right then, anyway.

Soon the brothers decided to focus on their big customers back east and leave Berkeley behind. With new suits, ninety dollars, and a back seat full of fluorescent inks and paints, Bob and Joe drove off to Ohio on New Year's Day 1936. There they settled in Cleveland and earned a living by providing colors for fluorescent posters. But they also kept chasing after better colors and new ideas, each brother in his own way.

Bob was a morning person, and Joe liked the night. Joe might wrap up his work and hit the hay not long before Bob awoke to begin his research. Bob focused on specific goals, while Joe let his freewheeling mind roam every which way when he tried to solve a problem. "If just one experiment out of a thousand succeeds," Joe would say, "then you're ahead of the game."

OHIO
2300 MILES

For Bob and Joe, the tough times of the Great Depression meant living and experimenting on the cheap. When Bob got married in 1936, his wife moved into the apartment the brothers were sharing. Patricia let Bob "borrow" her shiny satin wedding dress, and that was the last time she saw it in one piece.

After Joe got married in 1938, he and his wife, Elise, moved into a
run-down old farmhouse so he would have room for his own laboratory.
It wasn't the best place for a young family, as their baby boy liked to
chew on chemical-splattered shoes.

But Bob and Joe's efforts paid off brilliantly. One day they drove out to the city of Sandusky to check on a new billboard they had developed. Instead of using ink, they had soaked the billboard's fabric panels with a combination of fluorescent orange dye and hot alcohol. If the dye didn't fade too quickly, the ultraviolet lamps on the billboard would make for an eye-grabbing nighttime display.

When the billboard came into view that afternoon, what the brothers saw astonished them. From more than a mile away, it looked like the billboard was on fire!

When they got up close, the Switzers didn't find any flames. Instead they discovered something even more exciting. It was just like those silk samples Bob had seen in his backyard in Berkeley: even without the ultraviolet light on, the billboard was glowing—glowing bright orange in the setting sun.

By accident Joe and Bob had invented a totally new color. To their amazement it glowed in both daylight and ultraviolet light. They called this new color Fire Orange, and Joe used their newfound know-how to create other colors—glowing reds, yellows, greens, and more.

Meanwhile, Bob looked for ways these "Day-Glo" colors could be used. World War II provided lots of them.

Day-Glo fabric panels were used to send signals from the ground that could be seen by an airplane ten thousand feet in the air.

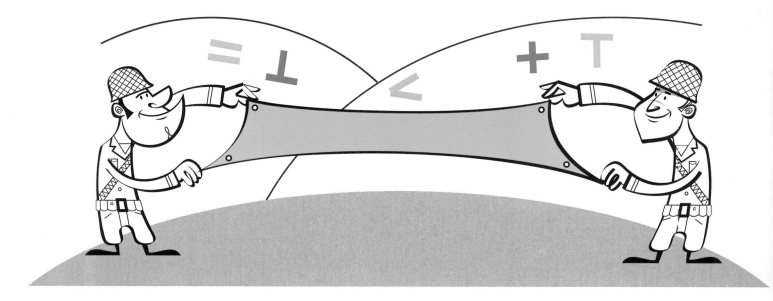

Survivors of disasters at sea used the panels in lifeboats to improve their chances of getting rescued.

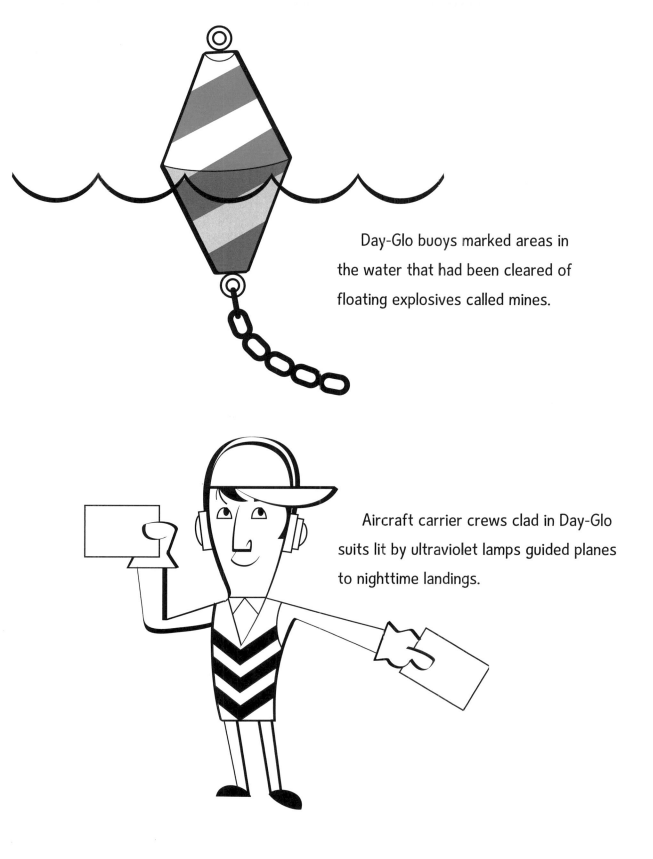

Day-Glo buoys marked areas in the water that had been cleared of floating explosives called mines.

Aircraft carrier crews clad in Day-Glo suits lit by ultraviolet lamps guided planes to nighttime landings.

In small but certain ways, the Switzers' inventions helped the United States and its allies win the war.

After the war Bob and Joe's colors made them rich. Day-Glo began to brighten everyday life back home. The colors made their way onto gas station signs and detergent boxes, traffic cones and magazine covers—including Joe's old favorite, *Popular Science.*

Artist Andy Warhol used them in his famous paintings. From life jackets to dump trucks, golf balls to goalposts, hula hoops to hunting vests, Joe and Bob's creations kept glowing and glowing.

When they were growing up, Bob and Joe Switzer wanted different things. Bob wanted to make his fortune by becoming a doctor, and Joe wanted to make his mark on the world through magic. At first it may seem that neither brother ended up where he wanted to be. But in that darkened basement, the Switzer brothers began to look at the world in a different light.

One brother wanted to save lives.
The other brother wanted to dazzle crowds.
With Day-Glo, they did both.

How Does Regular Fluorescence Work?

Sunlight is made up of colors ranging from red to violet. These colors combine to make white light. When white light hits an object, some of its colors are absorbed and some are reflected. In the case of, say, an orange, the color orange is reflected, and that's the color people see.

White light doesn't travel alone, though. Sunlight also carries invisible ultraviolet energy. The ultraviolet lamps that Joe Switzer read about in *Popular Science* use dark purple filters that hold back most white light and allow the invisible energy to pass through.

Instead of merely absorbing or reflecting ultraviolet, lots of minerals, chemicals, and other substances absorb this invisible energy and then release some of it as various colors of visible light— colors that glow in the dark.

This glowing effect is called fluorescence, and it is not visible in daylight. That's because regular reflected colors overpower the fluorescent ones.

How Does Daylight Fluorescence Work?

With daylight fluorescent colors, such as those sold under the Day-Glo name, white light boosts the fluorescence instead of overpowering it.

Just like an ordinary orange object, Bob and Joe Switzer's Sandusky billboard reflected the orange portion of the daylight and absorbed the other parts, including ultraviolet energy.

But the particular combination of dye and resin in the billboard's panels then released some of the absorbed daylight as additional orange light. Because the released light was the same color as the reflected light, the billboard gave off a lot more orange light than an ordinary orange object. That's what made it glow.

Go to **www.charlesbridge.com/day-glo-animation.html** to see an animation of how regular fluorescence and daylight fluorescence work.

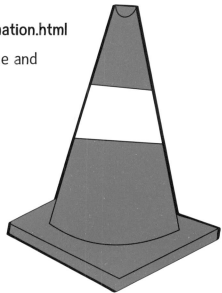

I have seen Day-Glo colors my whole life, but I had never considered how those colors came to be until Bob Switzer died in 1997 and I read his obituary in the *New York Times.* That article introduced me to Bob and Joe Switzer's story.

The story stuck with me, and when I began writing for children a few years later, it was one of the first ones I wanted to tell. But I needed more information about Joe and Bob, and I couldn't find any books about them. Bob's obituary gave the names of his surviving family members—Joe had died in 1973—so I found their phone numbers and began calling.

I received more cooperation from the Switzer family than I could have imagined. Bob's widow, Pat, and Joe's first wife, Elise de Groot, shared their memories with me, as did several of Bob's and Joe's children. I thank them all. My deepest appreciation goes to Bob and Joe's younger brother, Fred Switzer, who provided a wealth of information and guidance.

Of course, I wish I could have spoken with Joe and Bob themselves. In 1984, shortly before the Switzer family sold the Day-Glo Color Corp., Bob wrote by longhand a seventy-five-page history of their years before moving to Ohio. So I had Bob's version of events, but because Joe died relatively young and had never cared much for writing, his side of the story was harder to come by.

That's why nothing about this project meant more to me than the family's willingness to share Bob's and Joe's original letters, notes, and other materials detailing their earliest experiments and business successes. I majored in history in college, but I never felt so much like a true historian as when I held those seventy-year-old artifacts in my hands.

Beyond the Switzer family, I relied on many other sources, including:

> *The Story of Day-Glo,* a book self-published in
> 1991 by Switzer family friend Liesa Bing

 United States Patent 2,417,384, for the Switzers'
daylight fluorescent signaling and display device

 The US Army's historical office at Fort Monmouth,
New Jersey

> Bob and Joe's colleague Tom Gray, who shared the
> "flaming billboard" story

 The *Popular Science* article that got Joe going in the
first place

Inspired by that article, I bought an ultraviolet bulb and brought it
home to share with my family. It required no special filters—we just
screwed it into a desk lamp, hauled it into a closet, and turned it on
to see what we could see. My notes for this book were highlighted with
Day-Glo flags and markers. With that bulb, I had the thrill of watching
those colors radiate in the darkness—of seeing my research glow with
energy and life.